In the
stree

INTRODUCTION

Most of us live in towns and cities and we often take the roads and streets for granted. In every street there is something interesting – there are always people working, bus stops, lamps, shops, street notices, signs, vehicles and much, much more. Most of us take a journey that involves walking or driving along a street, it could be to school or to the park and more often than not we scarcely look around us. But even the most seemingly humdrum of workaday streets is full of interest if you keep your eyes open.

The things that you can spot on country roads will be different to what you can see in the towns and cities. It may be quite easy to see a horse and rider or village green in the countryside but quite difficult to find a grand town hall or multi-storey car park. There will be a lot more traffic in the towns and cities in the form of buses, taxis, cars and bicycles. Or some areas may be designated for pedestrians only.

Take your i-SPY In the Street with you when you are out visiting, shopping or on holiday, and seek out particular places of interest. We have given you plenty of examples here, but just look around you, about you, above your head and down to your feet, you'll be surprised at what you can see!

How to use your i-SPY book

As you work through this book, you will notice that the subjects are arranged in groups which are related to the kinds of places where you are likely to find things. You need 1000 points to send off for your i-SPY certificate (see page 64) but that is not too difficult because there are masses of points in every book. Each entry has a star or circle and points value beside it. The stars represent harder to spot entries. As you make each i-SPY, write your score in the circle or star. There are questions dotted throughout the book that can double your i-SPY score. Check your answers on page 63.

5

Points: 5

TRAFFIC LIGHTS

Traffic lights were invented in 1868 and were originally powered by gas. Today, they are controlled by computers and are used to regulate traffic on roads all over the world.

PELICAN CROSSING

Points: 5

5

A pelican crossing has a push button to control the traffic lights. When it is safe to cross, the green man sign is displayed and sometimes a bleep alarm sounds. 'Pelican' stands for PEdestrian LIght CONtrolled Crossing.

ZEBRA CROSSING

Points: 5

Black and white stripes on the road mean that drivers MUST stop to allow pedestrians to cross. Some zebra crossings have LOOK LEFT or LOOK RIGHT painted on the road to show which way the traffic is coming from.

Points: 10

LOLLIPOP PERSON

Lollipop ladies and men help children to cross busy roads on their way to and from school. The tall lollipop-shaped sign is bright yellow so that it stands out even on foggy days.

Points: 5

Railings are often positioned near pedestrian crossings to stop people stepping off the kerb. They direct them to the safest place to cross the road.

TACTILE PAVING

Points: 10

The raised pimples on the ground near a pedestrian crossing are known as 'tactile paving'. They warn people with poor eyesight that they are near the kerb.

Points: 15

BELISHA BEACON

Orange flashing lights on top of black and white striped poles warn motorists that a pedestrian crossing is ahead. The beacons are named after Leslie Hore-Belisha, the Minister of Transport who added beacons to pedestrian crossings in 1934.

BOLLARD

Points: 5

These white and yellow bollards light up at night to warn drivers that there is an obstacle or a crossing ahead.

Points: 25

AUTOMATIC BOLLARD

Some bollards can be lowered to allow certain vehicles to pass over them, then raised again to keep others out. They may be operated by a person in a control room or from transmitters placed on authorised vehicles, such as buses.

SPEED BUMP

Points: 5

Where cars move more slowly, there are fewer traffic jams and fewer serious accidents. Speed bumps have been installed on streets in many towns, especially close to schools, to slow cars down.

Points: 5

ZIGZAG LINE

5

White zigzagged lines on the road warn motorists not to park or overtake near a crossing. They help to ensure better visibility and safety around pelican and zebra crossings.

TRAFFIC CALMING

Points: 15

15

Making roads narrower for a short stretch forces cars to slow down, and makes it safer for pedestrians and other road users.

7

MANHOLE COVER

Points: 10

These circular metal lids can be lifted up to give workmen access to the drains and sewers that run underneath the road.

 Points: 5

DRAIN

When it rains, the water runs through the metal grilles and down into the drains. Without them, the road would flood!

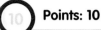

Points: 10

POT HOLE

Pot holes like this are often caused by rain and frost, which make the road surface crack open. They are particularly dangerous to motorcyclists and cyclists.

COBBLED STREET

Points: 20

Roads were covered by stone cobbles like these in Victorian times, and some can still be seen today. They can be very slippy when wet, so be careful.

UNDERGROUND PIPES/CABLES

Points: 20

Gas , electricity and water are carried to houses via pipes or cables that are buried underground. Sometimes these are exposed when they are being worked on.

 Points: 5

DOUBLE YELLOW LINES

Yellow lines at the edge of the road warn drivers not to park, load or unload their cars during the times indicated on the accompanying sign.

DOUBLE RED LINES

Points: 25

Some busy major routes in urban areas have double red lines, which mean that no-one can stop their vehicle at any time of the day or night. In this way, traffic can keep moving without stationary vehicles causing an obstruction.

Points: 25

WEATHER VANE

You may find a weather vane attached to the highest part of a building. These metal structures indicate the direction of the wind. There are many different shapes of weather vane.

SPEED CAMERA

Points: 10

Speed cameras detect vehicles that are going too fast. The camera takes an image of the moving vehicle and determines its speed. A fine may be issued to the driver.

TV AERIAL

Points: 5

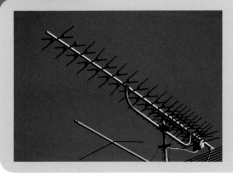

Traditional aerials are spikey and tend to be located on the sides of tall chimneys.

Points: 5

SATELLITE DISH

Satellite dishes are common on houses which have televisions with many different channels.

Points: 15

CCTV

CCTV cameras are often positioned high up on the side of buildings and record all the activity in the street below.

TELEGRAPH WIRES

Points: 15

Wooden telegraph poles carry telephone wires between properties. Look out for flocks of birds perched on them! Many telephone wires now run underground.

Points: 10

CHIMNEY

Chimneys on houses are usually made of brick. The clay pots that top the older chimneys are sometimes decorated with interesting designs.

BLUE PLAQUE

Top Spot!   **Points: 50** ⭐ 50

ENGLISH HERITAGE
JIMI
HENDRIX
1942~1970
Guitarist and
Songwriter
lived here
1968~1969

chrisdorney / Shutterstock.com

These plaques are put on to houses where someone famous once lived. You will find plaques for all sorts of people, from sportsmen and women to politicians, authors to musicians.

Write the name of the famous person on the blue plaque you saw:..
....

14

Points: 10

SCAFFOLDING

Scaffolding covers buildings that are under construction or renovation. They make it easier and safer for work to be done high up.

CRANE

Points: 25

Tall, skeletal cranes that tower over houses and buildings are used on building sites to move heavy loads.

 Points: 40 **Top Spot!**

CRANE SUPPORT

Large cranes need additional support feet to spread the heavy load above them and give them stability.

STREET LIGHTS

Points: 5

Street lights are operated with a light-sensitive timer, so they switch on automatically at dusk.

Points: 20

OLD-FASHIONED STREET LIGHTS

Some lights are an older style so they are suitable for historic areas. They look more like gas lamps.

ADVERTISING LIGHTS

Points: 20

Illuminated advertising signs brighten up a dull evening!

Points: 5

GUTTERING

Gutters carry rainwater away from the roofs of buildings and down into the drains. Old ones are generally made from cast iron and can be very decorative.

ROOFS

Points: 5

Roofs can be flat or pointed. Some have red tiles, others are covered in grey slate. If you can look down on a street from a high window, look at the jagged outline of many different-shaped buildings with all sorts of different coloured roofs.

TRAFFIC JAM

Points: 10

If you get stuck in a traffic jam, see what you can spy from the car window!

Points: 5

BUS STOP

You are bound to find a bus stop in a street near you...

OUT OF SERVICE BUS STOP

Top Spot! **Points: 35**

...but sometimes the bus stop may have to be taken out of service. This can happen if road works are being carried out.

This bus stop is not in use.

Points: 10

These are single-decker buses that can be found on more rural routes as well as in the city,

DOUBLE-DECKER BUS

Points: 10

Double-decker buses can carry lots of people at any one time. They are so tall that you can stand up on both the lower deck and the upper deck!

19

BENDY BUS

Their proper name is articulated bus. They consist of two separate sections linked by a pivoted joint which allows them to bend in the middle as they go round corners. They can be found at airports and in some cities.

Points: 30

TRAM

Trams run on rails through some city streets. Be careful to look both ways when you cross tram lines.

5 **Points: 5**

When the bus or tram doesn't go where you want to go, you might need to flag down a taxi. Taxis are often given their own lane in busy city streets so they can get around quickly.

Points: 5 **5**

With more cycle lanes on city streets than ever before, cycling has become a popular way to travel. Bikes come in all shapes and sizes, from sleek racing bikes to chunky all terrain machines. There are even some bikes that you ride while lying down!

MOTORCYCLIST

Points: 10

Look out for motorcyclists dressed in protective leather clothing.

Points: 30

FLAT TYRE

If you get a flat tyre, you'll have to stop – wherever you are!

Points: 25

SOFT TOP

With the roof rolled back, a ride in a convertible car is fun on a sunny day.

4X4 VEHICLE

Points: 10

Large four-wheel drive vehicles are easy to spot as they are higher than other cars.

RAILWAY STATION

Points: 10

There are more than 2,400 stations on Britain's railway network, ranging in size from great mainline terminals in cities, to small branch line stations in the middle of the countryside.

Points: 20

LEVEL CROSSING

Where a road crosses a railway line at a level crossing, barriers will be lowered to stop the cars and allow the train to pass. Always be careful at level crossings.

Points: 10

CAR PARK

Car parks are dotted around towns and cities. They can vary from large multi-storey buildings to small marked-out spaces.

TICKET MACHINE

 Points: 10

Don't forget to pay for a ticket from the machine when you park!

 Points: 15

PARKING METER

You'll usually find parking meters at the side of the road. They allow cars to be parked alongside them for a certain length of time.

PARKING TICKET

Points: 30

Oh dear! This driver is in for a nasty shock. If you fail to display the correct parking ticket, or exceed your time, it is likely that a parking ticket will be issued...

Points: 40 **Top Spot!**

CAR BEING TOWED AWAY

...and it is possible that the car could be towed away and impounded, which will be more expensive.

Emergency vehicles have fluorescent paintwork and blue flashing lights that make them easy to spot. If the siren is on, you will hear them coming!

Points: 10

Look carefully at the front of the car. 'POLICE' is written so drivers can read it correctly in their rear-view mirrors.

maryana / Shutterstock.com

AMBULANCE

Points: 10

The chequered pattern on some vehicles is known as 'battenburg' like the cake!

VanderWolf Images / Shutterstock.com

Points: 15

FIRE ENGINE

These vehicles have a large cab so that between 4 and 6 firefighters can travel in it.

GLASS CARRIER

Points: 30

Glaziers' vans have special fittings for carrying big panes of glass.

Points: 5

REFUSE LORRY

These lorries have special lifts on the back for emptying the bins into the interior.

Points: 25

Security vans, which carry money to banks, are made of toughened steel and glass to deter thieves.

REMOVAL VAN

Points: 25

These lorries have huge bodies to enable them to carry the maximum amount of furniture when people move house.

Points: 25

CONCRETE MIXER TRUCK

Watch the mixer carefully, and you will see that the drum rotates slowly so the concrete inside doesn't set.

POSTAL VAN

Points: 10

Vans are used by postal workers when emptying postboxes and making deliveries. They are especially useful in rural areas.

Claudio Divizia / Shutterstock.com

Points: 20

RECOVERY VEHICLE

If your car breaks down and can't be repaired at the roadside, it might be taken to a local garage by one of these trucks.

Gabor Tinz / Shutterstock.com

Points: 15

15

Philip Lange / Shutterstock.com

As many as ten cars can be transported on these vehicles, which are designed to carry as many as possible.

CHERRY PICKER

Points: 25

These small, mobile cranes allow workmen to reach street lighting and telegraph wires. They may also be used for putting up Christmas lights in the street.

UNDERGROUND SIGN

Points: 10

You will see this sign all over London. It is for the underground rail system, way below your feet. You will find other underground railways outside London. Look for the signs for the Tyne and Wear Metro, the Glasgow Underground, and Liverpool Merseyrail for the same points.

Points: 40   **Top Spot!**

MOBILE LIBRARY

These specially adapted trucks carry a selection of books and provide library services for people who live in remote areas or who have difficulty accessing the library.

Points: 10

10

WOODEN FOOTPATH SIGN

PUBLIC FOOTPATH

Country signs are often made from wood rather than metal, and can be more in keeping with the surroundings.

VILLAGE GREEN

Points: 25

The centre of many villages is the green, usually near a crossroads or junction.

Claudio Divizia / Shutterstock.com

HALF-TIMBERED HOUSE

Points: 25

One way to spot a very old house is to look out for the wooden frame, which is usually brown or black. These timbers are often anything but straight!

Points: 30

THATCHED COTTAGE

The roofs on these traditional houses are made of reeds, straw or rushes. There are more thatched roofs in the United Kingdom than in any other European country.

Points: 10

PUB SIGN

Look out for interesting pub names and unusual pub signs. Write the most unusual name you have found here: ....
....

CHURCH

Points: 10

Parish churches are among the oldest buildings in the country. There are many different styles and some have amazing stained glass windows.

SCHOOL

Points: 15

Village schools often incorporate several different styles of building, from Victorian to modern.

Points: 25

VILLAGE HALL

The centre of the village community is usually the village hall, with a notice board to advertise what is going on.

Points: 25

HORSES ON THE ROAD

Spotting a horse on the street in an urban environment is unusual. You are more likely to find one on a country lane – the perfect place to go for a ride.

VILLAGE FAIR

Top Spot! Points: 40

Village fairs used to be the highlight of the summer, and they are still lots of fun to go to.

Traffic signs show speed limits and warn motorists and pedestrians of hazards ahead.

SPEED LIMIT

Points: 5

A sign with a red circular outline is an order sign and must be obeyed. In this case you must not go above the speed shown.

 Points: 10

CYCLE LANE

Information signs are rectangular. Many of them are blue.

ROUNDABOUT

Points: 10

Triangular signs give a warning of something ahead on the road.

Points: 15

PEDESTRIAN ZONE

Cars and motorcycles are not permitted in pedestrian zones, either permanently or at certain times of the day.

SCHOOL

Points: 10

Drivers are warned to slow down as they approach a school.

TOWN NAME

Points: 10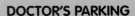

As you enter a town or village, its name is displayed on a sign so you know where you are

Points: 25

DOCTOR'S PARKING

Doctors may use these designated parking areas provided they have the correct permit. This saves time if they need to attend emergencies.

HOUSE NUMBER

Some houses have painted tiles or signs showing their number...

Points: 5

HOUSE NAME

...and some houses have no number at all, just a name!

Points: 10

OLD STREET NAME

Street names often indicate what was made or sold there in the past.

Points: 25

STRANGE STREET NAME

Look out for strange street names. Write the most unusual you can find:.................................
....

Top Spot! **Points: 35**

MULTIPLE SIGN

Points: 20
double for a multiple sign
with six or more signs

These signs show many different places of interest.

Points: 15

NO LITTER

This sign tells you not to drop any litter on the ground, but to put it in the bin and keep the environment tidy.

Points: 10

SKIP

Builders need skips – big metal containers – to clear away rubble and rubbish from building sites.

ROAD WORKS

Points: 10

Road works usually mean improvements are being made to the road or pipework, but they can also mean delays and traffic jams.

Points: 15

PUBLIC TOILET

A relief to those in need, but watch out because sometimes you need to pay to 'spend a penny'!

43

WALL POSTBOX

Points: 25

Postboxes set in to walls were once a common sight, less so today...

Points: 5

POSTBOX

...but the red pillar box is a more familiar sight on British streets. The first postbox in Britain was erected in 1852.

TELEPHONE BOX

Points: 30

Telephone boxes are gradually disappearing from British streets, as most people now have mobile phones. The old red boxes are becoming harder to find.

Points: 5

LITTER BIN

In many places litter bins now have several different slots so that rubbish can be sorted and recycled more easily. Always put litter in the bins provided.

GRIT BOX

Points: 15

Big yellow boxes at the roadside store grit which can be spread on the roads during winter to melt the ice.

Points: 10

NEWSPAPER BOARD

Boards outside newsagents advertise the news headlines.

TOWN HALL

Points: 15

The Town Hall is usually centrally located and is often a grand building.

 Points: 5

BENCH

You may want to take a rest from walking or shopping; what better place than a bench to rest on.

FLOWERS ON LAMP-POST

Points: 20

Flowers always brighten up the street!

Points: 15

FOUNTAIN

Fountains can vary from very elaborate structures with statues, to more simple water features.

BICYCLES FOR HIRE

Points: 25

In some cities, you can hire a bike for the afternoon.

Points: 5

SHOPPING TROLLEY

Look out for these at supermarkets. Many supermarkets charge a small refundable deposit to use them – this stops people pushing them all the way home!

STATUE

Points: 15

Statues often commemorate important people or events and give you a chance to learn about the local history. Write the name of the historical figure you saw as a statue here:...
....

48

Points: 15

LIBRARY

Larger villages and towns usually have a place where you can borrow books and use a computer to access the internet.

CASHPOINT

Points: 5

You can take money out of your bank account at a cashpoint. You will find these at banks and also at some newsagents, petrol stations and supermarkets.

Points: 10

RECYCLING POINT

Separate bins are used to sort all the things that can be recycled.

Town centres usually have a number of shops. Some will sell just one type of thing, such as bread or meat, while larger shops may sell a variety. Other shops sell a service, such as hairdressers. Look out for corner shops and rows of local shops too.

BUTCHER

Points: 10

Butchers prepare fresh cuts of meat for sale. Some specialise in meat for particular cultural requirements.

Points: 10

BAKER

A baker traditionally bakes bread, but a bakery usually sells cakes and pastries too and some have a café.

FISHMONGER

Points: 15

Fishmongers sell raw fish and seafood such as crab and lobster.

COFFEE SHOP/CAFÉ

Points: 5

TEA ROOM

Points: 15

SANDWICH SHOP

Points: 10

ICE CREAM SHOP

Points: 20

KEY CUTTING SHOP

Points: 10

If you need a new key this shop can help!

Points: 10

SHOE SHOP

Do you like to shop for new shoes?

CLOTHES SHOP

Points: 10

What about new clothes? There are many different types of clothes shops to choose from.

Points: 5

CHEMIST

Most chemists dispense medicines, but you can also buy toothpaste, shampoo, plasters and many other things too.

BANK

Points: 5

If the bank is closed you can still get cash from the machine.

Points: 10

POST OFFICE

The Post Office doesn't just sell stamps. They offer lots of different services.

INDIAN RESTAURANT

Points: 10

CHINESE RESTAURANT

Points: 10

ITALIAN RESTAURANT

Points: 10

CHIP SHOP

Points: 5

ANTIQUE SHOP

Points: 25

BOOKSHOP

Points: 15

FLORIST

Points: 10

CHARITY SHOP

Points: 5

SWEET SHOP

Points: 20

CAKE SHOP

Points: 15

BARBER (WITH STRIPY POLE)

Points: 20

HAIRDRESSER

Points: 5

GREENGROCER

Points: 15

SUPERMARKET

Points: 5

CAR SHOWROOM

Points: 10

PETROL STATION

Points: 5

There are a surprising number of uniforms to spot on the street – see how many you can find.

HOTEL PORTER

This one is particularly smart!

 Top Spot! Points: 40

POSTMAN/POSTWOMAN

Points: 5

TRAFFIC WARDEN

Michal Kowalski / Shutterstock.com

Points: 10

POLICE OFFICER

Points: 15

58

Look out for these people while you are out and about.

SUPERMARKET DELIVERY PERSON

Points: 10

ROAD WORKER

Points: 10

WINDOW CLEANER

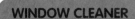

Points: 15

ROAD CLEANER

Points: 20

PAINTER/DECORATOR

Points: 20

MARKET TRADER

Points: 10

BUSKER

Points: 15

SKATEBOARDER

Points: 20

Points: 40 **Top Spot!**

STREET ARTIST

Some street artists create original works, while others copy the Old Masters.

STREET PERFORMER

Points: 20

What do you like to watch? Acrobatics balloon twisting, mime and caricature drawing are only a few of the performance arts to spot.

Points: 15

STREET FOOD SELLER

Are you hungry? Street food varies from ice cream in summer to hot roast chestnuts in winter, but many sites sell drinks, sandwiches, or hot food all year.

TOWN CRIER

artistan / Shutterstock.com

Town criers, with their traditional colourful outfits, are sometimes found in older cities and towns. In the past, the town crier would ring his bell and shout the daily news loud enough for the whole town to hear!

INDEX

i-SPY

How to get your i-SPY certificate and badge

Let us know when you've become a super-spotter with 1000 points and we'll send you a special certificate and badge!

HERE'S WHAT TO DO!

NO LITTERING

- ✓ Ask an adult to check your score.

- ✓ Visit www.collins.co.uk/i-SPY to apply for your certificate. If you are under the age of 13 you will need a parent or guardian to do this.

- ✓ We'll send your certificate via email and you'll receive a brilliant badge through the post!